Where Scars Become Stars

Diyasha Mukherjee

India | USA | UK

Copyright © Diyasha Mukherjee
All Rights Reserved.

This book has been self-published with all reasonable efforts taken to make the material error-free by the author. No part of this book shall be used, reproduced in any manner whatsoever without written permission from the author, except in the case of brief quotations embodied in critical articles and reviews.

The Author of this book is solely responsible and liable for its content including but not limited to the views, representations, descriptions, statements, information, opinions, and references ["Content"]. The Content of this book shall not constitute or be construed or deemed to reflect the opinion or expression of the Publisher or Editor. Neither the Publisher nor Editor endorse or approve the Content of this book or guarantee the reliability, accuracy, or completeness of the Content published herein and do not make any representations or warranties of any kind, express or implied, including but not limited to the implied warranties of merchantability, fitness for a particular purpose.

The Publisher and Editor shall not be liable whatsoever...

Made with ❤ on the BookLeaf Publishing Platform
www.bookleafpub.in
www.bookleafpub.com

Dedication

To everyone I love,
to every version of myself I have outgrown,
& to every soul who has stitched
light into their wounds.

This book is yours.

Preface

This book is a constellation of moments—
fragments of feeling, whispers of the soul, and the quiet
light that emerges from shadow.
These poems are born of scars: the hidden aches, the
trembling vulnerabilities and the small,
miraculous ways we endure them.
Here, every wound becomes a star, every fracture a
spark, illuminating the dark spaces within us.
Read these pages slowly, and let the words settle like
stardust in your heart.

This is a space to feel, to remember, and to heal.
This is **where scars become stars.**

Acknowledgements

This book would not exist without the quiet voices that have shaped me—those who whispered courage into my ear when I thought I could not rise, and those who taught me that even pain can be a teacher.

To my family and loved ones: thank you for your patience, your warmth, and for holding space for the storms and the silences that birthed these words.

To every soul who has ever felt loss, longing, or the weight of unseen scars: your resilience inspired these pages. You are the constellations in my poems, the stars I could not have found alone.

To the poets, writers, and dreamers who came before me: thank you for showing me that words can carry light into the dark corners of the heart.

To the Almighty: thank you for the breath that fills these pages, for guiding my steps through shadow and light, and for planting the stars that shine through my scars.

And finally, to myself—past, present, and future—for choosing to walk the path of feeling, of noticing, and of transforming scars into stars.

This book is a journey, and I am grateful to every heart that walks along with it.

1. Aviothic Haze

The clock says it's one in the morn',
I say I am yet to go down.
You see, places aren't places you are at night —
Conscience doesn't convocate with your sight.
I lay low within the waterspout,
Or I stay where I get shipwrecked.
The sky hears my prayers ricochet,
My wristlet's gold fades away —
There my silence lays.
Now the quilt smells like me,
My windows stay cold.
Aviothic haze hovers down my spine,
Till it pries the stars to unfold.
I am not there if the birds don't chirp,
If the rivers don't ripple,
If the inked feather doesn't scribble.
I'm only in the shadows —
In the meadows where the doves die.
I bury them.
I know they aren't phoenix;

They don't rise from ashes — they're reborn.
New air thrusts against their skin,
They fly over valleys where the world has never been.
I lay there.
I wave, I stay, I pray.
I rest where the meadows feel homely.
I choose to walk alone, not to walk lonely.

2. Ricochet

The ease of laughter swiftly fades away,
And then it feels like work -- hardwork.
One moment you are ensconced to the core,
The next, you find yourself detached from the earth.

You feel mellow in the yellow twilights,
As the sun rises in the eyes of a mage,
You find your chest weighing more than usual,
As the sun sets in your ribcage.

Well, you are a wallflower from within,
But you completely forget that for a while,
Not a single wandering ponder you see,
'Cause you have painted daisies on your smile.

But when you stroll through a beautiful hallway,
And you reflect daisies on the chandelier,
You suddenly hit the ground of reality,
And shed nectars of wallflower through your tears.

Then you finally ask yourself the reason —
'Cause it's easier when there's a corner for the sun to set.
When no answers come, no voice, no explanation,
Only a halo of nothing is all you get.

So you see —
You've cut through bullets,
You've been through wars,
You've painted your casket,
You've embellished your scars,
You've wept an ocean —
But never your guard.

Then tell me,
How could nothingness ricochet this hard?

3. River Down A Reverie

River down a reverie,
When you're low and stakes are high,
When all the glasses shatter,
Through the crest of all's despise.

River down a reverie,
When the soul has been maimed,
Try to put it back together,
To the frame where it first rained.

River down a reverie,
When amity turns blue,
When the true sun flowers, mirage as roses to all,
Where you're losing you.

River down a reverie,
When the storm caves in,
When it wrecks the little valley,
Of all the serenity you had within.

So my girl,
From all that's been gained,
To all that ends up lost,
Do not unlearn to stand alone,
At any time, at any cost.
Don't forget to rise from ashes,
Don't forget to show some bravery,
When that's all you're left with —
Honey, river down a reverie.

4. Where the Waters Stop Flowing

I see the air settle down where the waters stop flowing,
The night steals the humid tears away.
I lone myself in the same pyre I burn in.
The corners of the verandah fixed with my spine,
I walk on the gripless floor,
I follow the raindrops through the mesh.
Trip with all the weight of diffidence in my heart.
I fall, flawed, in my own dehiscent flesh.
Then times when I uncouth all I don't have within,
When I rip a part of you and me,
I hope you carry enough to confront me open.
I hope you bury the mesh down the mud.
I hope you cohere the real parts of me that
aren't yet broken.
And in the next sunrise, when I fall back again,
And the pyre swallows me whole,
Hum the lullaby I slept to last night to.
I'll crawl back to the lap I rest in—
This time not a fire I'll burn in,

But a sea I'll float into.
For I promise, when I'm not myself again,
This time I'll crawl back dripping in more love than I already do.
So when I make a fist this time,
Hold me hard, just once more.
When I push a fight,
Pull me to your chest, just once more.
When I fail to be a part of the constellation that you can't look up to,
Don't stop looking for me, Just once more,
And when I try to rip a part of you and me again,
Please love me harder than you already do—
Just once more.

5. When the Midnight Hits the Dorm

When the midnight hits the dorm,
I miss my mom a little more.
When the morning rays touch the drapes,
And Mom calls me up to say,
"Good morning, baby, begin the day!"
I miss her morning kisses on my face.

When it's 1 p.m. and lunch gets grabbed,
She calls me up in just a snap.
She orders, "Eat properly, don't miss that!"
While herself refusing all the delicacies that I can't have.

Times when the lectures are done,
Everyone rushes onto a joyous run.
I, on the other hand, ache in melancholy,
'Cause when I'm back to the dorm room,
There's no Mum.

Some might ask, "Why are you so homesick?

What's so much in your hometown to utter?"
I can't help but explain this simple thing:
My home is not my hometown — my home is my father and mother.

Apparently,
The night caves in and I'm back to the same form.
I think of all the years I've spent before,
And just when the midnight hits the dorm,
I miss my mom a little more.

6. The Fairy Lantern

My virgin leaves hold on with as much strength as the sunrays scatter at night.
My roots caress the earth with no need to hold on tight,
My withered petals trace the soil with tender embrace,
Unbound by the sheer need for a permanent place.

'Cause I am the wallflower — I'm not seen, you see?
While the orchids and the lilies get jostled, not free.
'Cause they seldom know how I look when I bloom,
They seldom consider to make me room.
'Cause those nurseries flourish, their colours painted bright and high,
For my hues bring colour only to the sky.
So I wait till all my leaflets wither away and die,
While I paint down the twilight, and go lost beyond the night.

For I am the fairy lantern — my identity, not shame,
But I bet till now, you probably didn't even know my name.

7. A Small Town Girl

You flee out of a room full of people,
Perhaps you breathe a few where you're not seen.
You're aubade — you're not evergreen,
You shed when all go free.
Sometimes when it hits rock bottom,
The seashells find their way back to the waters.
The night sweeps away the light,
And your words break enough to run dry.
You kneel into the shadows where your soul shatters,
You collect the shells and make a wristlet,
Wear it over — golden and pink,
A little star drooping down the rim.
Felt new for a while, felt seen,
But one day the star falls down,
The gold goes brown,
The shells break to the ground.
But your wrist? It's naked now.
You pick up your bag and leave —
You're done with new chapters, this time,
A new story.

A small-town girl with a soft heart,
Layers of hue laid beneath the skin.
The dove flies away when told she sinned,
There lays the dark innocence.
An old dungeon with a rusty lock,
Words of faults echo within —
From walls to the iron bars,
From the ground to the ceiling,
There she screams.
She runs from one corner to the other,
She begs for air but the echoes go up.
The voices become noises,
Her virtues become vices,
And she goes shut.

Now she realises,
She'd better have had a heart made of rock.
A small-town girl with a weak heart,
But now, a wooden cover laid upon the view.
Reasons are different to shed a tear,
But the extent of pain — nothing new.

8. Ashes of Expectations

Time.
A frame that locks the time,
The days that drool over dark skies,
Sometimes bind you.
One's merry hymn to a child's cry,
Where there are expectations along with faith,
Where you're present but not yet—
That's when you count upon time.
But have you been told what comes along?
What caves in and breaks you,
What stays in and never heals?
What wrecks your guts and makes you kneel?

Attachment.
The omnipresent opines:
May all souls learn to differ,
May none of you ever suffer,
May all of you learn the laws deeper and deeper,
That—
Attachment's an illusion.

It sweeps in swiftly and confines you deeply.
It makes you warm among people,
It makes you depend and bend.
You unlearn to stand alone,
Your toes freeze to the core.
You're then brushed away to the shore.
That's when you find yourself—
Alone, so alone.

Then you read the pages back.
You see,
Your footprints didn't touch the virgin grass,
Didn't cripple the new snow,
Didn't let the emotions flow.
It all came down to sunken rust—
All you were stepping on, was dust.
That dust is attachment.
Ashes of expectations,
Mirage as love for all,
'Cause attachment peaks at pain—
Pain of entitlement and expectations,
Pain of possession and right,
Pain of the thought of losing everyone,
At a single sight.
That's when you go home to the afterglow.
You let the night stay outside the window.
You hush your breath; you sit straight.

You feel the omnipresent in your veins,
In your heart and unsmiled lips.
But this time, you smile.
Hereafter, you glare at the dark sky outside,
Like attachment trying to cave in—
But now you're complete from within.
Now you wait for the dawn.

Once again, you count upon time.
But now,
You're aware of what you perceive.
You know what you must.
You know where your love for all stands firm,
And where lies the cloud of dust.

9. Childish River

Let there be grass greener on both the sides,
A childish river laughing at the sky.
Let the honeydews escape the shades,
Parade through those darkened days,
When there's seldom time to suffice—
The need to defy,
All that has been unearned,
Unlearned without the thought of time.
Then I shall plant a few daisies on your field,
I shall invite those fireflies,
Home them up in that little glass urn,
Freedom to be given to them as a return.
Then, when the sun gets tired of leading the day
And leaves the day behind,
You'll find the fireflies whisk away your mind,
Whisk away the shadow of the sky,
Fallen apart on your doorstep.
You'll find your daisies blooming,
You'll find the little girl in you beaming with a smile.
In joy, she'll tiptoe bare feet,

Dwindling all over,
Leaving those little fireflies straying behind.
Her nights wouldn't depend on them anymore—
She'd love the earth as much at night as in the day.
She'd bask under the sunlight,
River down the river like a paper boat on a rainy night.
It's when she'd finally be able to convey:
"Let there be grass greener on both the sides,
Let the blind dove catch a few shades of hue,
Let the childish river now laugh at the sky—
Till there's no time when there's you without you."

10. Tiptoe

Tiptoes over my sand dune,
And I was on the edge.
The sea roared at my shipwrecked boat,
To scrape away me to the shore,
For the weakened shoulders couldn't take anymore.
The ivory sky was long gone for sure.

Blood soaked in the crease of my palms,
I shed with every tear.
I made the sea the boat died in,
I watched me go away with fear.

Heavy was the pain of the never-ending ache,
For I didn't know how to float.
Either I could learn to breathe in the waters,
Or choose to die along my shipwrecked boat.

So I splattered around till the sand hit my toes,
I breathed in air and left the sea.
My skin burned and my soul unturned,

For my broken shoulders could no longer carry me.

Now I run barefoot by the waters,
Burn my eyes under the scorching noon.
I was on the edge when I gripped sand,
And laid my soul over the sand dune.

And when the weight brought me to my knees,
To teach my body for the pain to run,
The wave of woe went beyond my neck,
So I tiptoed over the sand dune till I was gone.

11. How Could I?

You fear I'll go,
No, not under some other sky,
Not like a stranger yearning to thrive,
You fear a pale skin of mine,
You fear that one day, I shall die.

Well I do, well I will, O I must,
But there's one thing you must trust,
I'm not going any time soon,
Not until the world learns to roar how much I love you.

Not until we've cried through nights,
Surviving ebbs and flows,
Learning saving people's lives.
Not until you confide your hues in my book,
The book of turning and freezing times,
Not until I flare into your arms,
Go mighty about the moments we froze,
Not until you cascade that vermilion,
Till it falls on the tip of my nose,

I'm not lying,
Dont worry, not at all any time soon,
I'm not dying.

Not until we build our own throne,
Not until we carry kids of our own,
You see, I have my life left for you,
The crest of my smiles inscribed for you,
How could I make things go blue,
Already this day or any time soon?
I have vallies of dreams marching on your way,
How could I march past them this noon?
I'm not going away so soon,
I'm not at all going away so soon.

But one day I will & when I do,
I need my loved ones safe and sound,
Lifeful and holding me around,
You'll be there, my head on your lap,
I'll keep the best parts of me for you to map.
But hey, that's a long time away,
Swing me around, keep your worries at bay,
I'm not at all leaving this full moon,
I'm not going away so soon.

Still Yes,
You fear that I'll go,

Not under some other sky,
Or a stranger yearning to thrive,
You fear a pale skin of mine.
But for once, see through my eyes,
A loving husband and a marvellous life,
Families bonding underneath the sky,
Embracing your lover after saving peoples lives,
Still For every time you think, soon I wanna die,
Dear Husband, How could I?

12. Dusked Fate

Shame,
It doesn't shed in tears, you see—
It remains.
Deep, where your mind can't comprehend.
I have felt shame with profoundness,
I awe over how firmly it holds itself within you.
You spill over vices and pay numerous prices,
But shame—it rains.
You try somnolence, but it fails.
The bird inside that rib cage flutters,
You stutter down the road.
There, the polaroids burn—
The moments, the happy ones, they don't return.
Echoes shoot behind that rat inside your head,
Die in thirst of giving it all away.
But shame still smiles,
crooked the corner it makes,
It grins at your dusked fate,
Ruins all the praises you get.
And now, you're resistant,

You're incapable of smiles and tears.
You're detached from your heart,
Even after all it bears.
You still can't cry a single tear.
That tear remains, that tear is pain.
That pain could make the lion shed all of his mane.
That pain, when it hails down on your cold chest—
My dear,
You manage to find some traces of my shame.

13. Illicit Caves

I cannot anymore.
I cannot live with her anymore.
She is present and absent, both at the same time.
She darkens her eyes in a room full of light.
She has lost all of her might to be able to fight.
She was gone before she confronted her mind.

I cannot live with her anymore,
'Cause she is loud.
She is red in unseen blood.
She hurts the people she chose to love.
She repents her actions,
She repents her words.

I cannot live with her anymore,
'Cause her heart runs faster than time.
She turns faceless, nameless, ruthless, and naïve.
She stabs me over and over—
In a silent crime.

I cannot live with her anymore,
'Cause she's only livable when she's asleep—
When her shameless anxiety forgets to beep,
When she forgets to kill me, forgets to creep
Into all those illicit caves she wasn't meant to see.

I cannot live with her anymore.
But now I'm afraid— I'm drowning in the sea
Of the truth I cannot happen to skip.
Now I stand alone, with the truth freezing my feet:
That I'm no one else but her, & she is no one else but me.

14. The Call I Couldn't Make

Today, when the time struck my heart,
When the last bit of my spine tore apart,
When I didn't know how to start,
I picked up the dial.
I called my father,
I mouthed a "hello" but couldn't proceed further.

I couldn't tell him that his strong daughter was now tired —
Tired of all that she had endured,
Tired of all the innumerable bruises,
That she'd crash onto the stones every time she loses.
That she feels her heart break,
With every beat she loses strength.
The world curses her to shed,
Into a damsel she wasn't meant to be made.

She hurts, Father — I hurt badly.
I hurt, and it kills me... but doesn't really.
It only makes me feel death, but it doesn't stop.

I carry the baggage of humiliation every time I drop.

I am tired, Father — I need your arms.
The world has failed your baby,
Now she sleeps with blood on her palms.
She cries for you, but she knows you'd get scared —
If only you had known what all she had dared.

If only her silent cries roared into your sky,
If only her timid bliss was able to thrive,
If only she'd confide in how she walks on the cold earth,
If only she could accept being just a piece of dirt.
If only all of the pains she'd gained could be cured,
Father — she'd surely own a medal for all she has endured.

15. Woodlore

For once my eyes saw what my heart sees:
On your front porch, me, holding on to the keys,
You and your maimed blue heart,
Remained buried deep inside the backyard.
I unearth,
Your wooden heart was now cold sore,
And I wasn't a Woodlore.

16. On This Long Dark Street

Small talks are too deep to be sent,
Small hearts are hard to melt,
Small tries feel worthless to seek,
'Cause they couldn't hear the way you felt.

I hummed my song in your heart,
Touched your soul, when time kept us apart,
I turned, dropped two bricks on my rib,
Shook my heart, forcing it to beat.

I coloured your soul — black, white, and blue,
But I was so lost in my inner turmoil,
That I couldn't comprehend you.

You curled your lips away from mine,
I was locked behind the bars of time,
My sobbing face threw a flash of a smile,
But you held your arms for her — she looked fine.

I guess now I can say that you love her,
But I was always sure that you loved me —
   You loved me the way I wanted it,
      So deep, that I couldn't see.

   So today, on this long dark street,
   As the wet road lay beneath my feet,
  Today I've forgotten if I have a heart,
Or have forgotten the way it used to beat.

17. Let The Love Bend

Let the love bend,
Make sure it doesn't shed,
Onto the ground full of dead petals.

What's that ivory purity?
What's with that ego-painted dignity?
It's all an illusion,
It all sheds where the pain cripples.

But did the love shed?
I hope it didn't.
I hope it consumed every single vice,
I hope you found peace without paying a price.

I hope your love is like that—
Hopeless, selfless, endless.

So don't worry, my dear,
Let your love bend,
Just make sure it doesn't shed,

That it doesn't fade.
If still not broken,
It wasn't meant to break.

18. Ivy & Her Friends

Here comes our little Ivy,
Piercing through the not-so-little world.
She has her music cassettes lined on her desk,
And her sorrows perfectly hurled.

Little Ivy sits against the Christmas tree,
She has her friends around her.
Ivy loves to braid one of their hairs,
And murmur her silliest fantasies to those
Who surround her.

One of them — Blair, as she was called —
Would get on and help adorn the Christmas tree.
Jadey and Nelle would stand on either side,
And help them stand firm on their knees.

Over there,
Owen and Charlie would gaze into the stars
Long before the fairy lights were up.
Ivy would giggle in mere desperation,

"You see, stars are the scars the galaxy couldn't cover up."

Soon it hit ten, and the neighbours called her upon.
They all said Ivy was too much into her mind,
"Oh, she has a fantasy full of companies she's down for,
And roams around with stories no matter what she finds."

Little Ivy, Oh our little Ivy,
She must face the bite of the thorny wars.
It's time she comes out strong and bright,
For she is not a cloudless sky —
But a constellation of a million stars.

But they don't know how she needs a Blair,
They don't know she needs a Jadey and a Nelle to hold her stay put.
They don't know she yearns for an Owen and a Charlie to gaze upon her stars,
To heal her scars — she couldn't cut from the root.

19. Blythe

5th December

"She is Blythe, too bizarre," they whispered.
But I whirled the certainty to be questionable,
As she adorned her gazes in a hidden whim,
That now made her existence unignorable.

She walked into the room, she borrowed the keys,
She hemmed them and opened the door with ease,
She pried the bookshelves to find the one,
To read the words from where the tale had begun.

She sat on the bench, hair falling on her cheeks,
She tucked them behind her ears and flipped through pages in peace.
She chuckled at a moment, then looked away thereafter
—
I'd swear I'd never heard such honey laughter.

Then the bell rang and she hurried to class,

And she smiled in approach as she saw me pass.
I ruined the moment, I started trembling,
So she patted my back, and my senses began assembling.

Then she sat alone, and I found her under my surveillance,
So I approached her myself and saw her smile in silence.
She let me sit close but stayed quiet & serene,
So my only hope began perishing therein.

But today Blythe is leaving, far away—
I don't know if she would have ever wanted to stay.
She came out of nowhere for the final goodbye,
And I was trying my best not to cry.

As I saw her moon face for the last time,
I handed her my letter with a trembling sigh.
I stared into her eyes, but I got so nervous—
Surely, I could have kissed her then, on purpose.

But I walked out, my feelings hiding,
As I saw my written lines started confiding.
For the first time I second guessed and tore in terror,
But then I saw her sun-kissed face in the side-view mirror.

For she read,

What my letter said:

"Blythe, I'm that weird guy, if you remember,
Whom you saw in that library this December.
I'd hope for nothing more but you to come back soon,
And bring me my heart back that went along with you.
Blythe, I think I'm in love with you, but I am not broken,
So I promise I'll always keep my door open.
And now I would crave for nothing more,
But to relive the way you came and left my door."

Oh, her wet tears on that dry note,
Lay in layers under her sun-drunk tone,
Made a montage of moments that had crept in—
Stayed scattered like new snow until she wept in.

20. Shed Lilies

Wouldn't say all my life,
But my life has dealt with the dark—
A scorching flare of burn in the chest,
Over a haunting shadow, it would lark.

I've been young on the face, really,
But I am old enough to pry the pain.
The social courtroom ain't my home, O Lord,
Please help me walk out of this midnight rain.

The ground has a grip on my ribs these days;
For one doesn't know the smile full of sorrow.
I shall continue to do my duties, O Lord,
But promise me—you'll bring me a better tomorrow.

I learn and unearth, unearth and learn—
Will the learning ever come to an end?
You see, O Lord, it's too hard to calm the waves,
With the sole rule to never let your morals bend.

I know it's not dark really, O Lord,
But the path that leads to the light.
But what to do when you're broken enough,
Or torn enough to be able to fight?

But before the fall, there was summer,
And before summer, there was spring—
A place full of yellow lilies and tulips,
A place where my girlhood could sing.

Thereby,
Wouldn't say all my life,
But my life has dealt with quite the pain—
A frozen ground full of shed lilies,
Where the weary dove could never fly again.

21. Life, Can You Hear Me?

Life, can you hear me?
Yes you do, you've always done.
You're brave and render around my sun.
But Life, do you hear my sound?
The pleads I don't plea,
The tears I can't free,
Life, can't you see?
My ribs have broken into pieces,
Scattered over the creases of my forehead,
Life, can't you touch?
Can't you pat my back, mend my chest?
With those broken ribs, can't you built a nest?
A nest, where I can lay and you can stay,
For I promise we both would pray, everyday,
For us to thrive into an oblivion,
Be gone from where it had begun.

19 years of life, and you think you know me?
Maybe you've touched my doorstep,
But you're still on the front porch,

Picking pebbles to break in.
Life, you don't know me from within.
But the omnipresent does,
And I know you're afraid enough to answer,
'Cause when she handed my soul onto you,
You promised to take care,
But you don't.
You're still busy picking pebbles.
Maybe you don't have to break in,
Maybe all you have to do, is to knock the door,
That I don't happen to open anymore.

But life, you stay back!
You didn't listen to your karma,
You won't listen to me.
You won't fathom your own words,
You won't set me free.
Life, you are just a need,
To stay, to be,
Where people forget people,
And the morals they would preach.
Life you should know,
This is a karmic debt you'll pay,
Not an evening show.
By now, you should learn to bow.
For all the lines you've crossed by now.

Life, you're wrecked.
You made my tears tired enough to shed.
For all those times I crooned you to cradle my head,
To all those expectations that you haven't met,
You're a bane to me, You've abandoned me,
You vex till my feet burn underneath.
You better stay out that door,
Till the dusts mirage against your theft,
I shall leave you, before nothing remains left.
Cause You've made me loose people,
People I were made of,
People I loved.
'Cause She still lives across the street but refuses to recognize me,
Maybe one still savors those vanilla biscuits underneath the school's garden tree,
One still fights with wooden rulers to rule the kingdoms we built,
One still endorses ignorance without a tint of guilt.

But life, I don't.
I still remember those bricks I made that broke my spine,
The parts of childhood I rave and have locked in time,
The sunny sundays and those chilly birthdays,
Life you were pretty beautiful before you decayed.
But Life, I've got only a few of 'em left,
By now, You better start knocking on that door,

You better start mending my chest,
Before I'm gone enough to open anymore.

22. Fluent in Silence

Silence,
She lays where I turn cold,
Where the sky sheds dew,
Where my eyes turn dry,
When the universe couldn't know why.
Silence pricks my unseen scars,
Pricks all the demons inside me,
Pricks the little girl out of her closet,
Till those tears go dry enough to confide in me.
Silence is beautiful, you see,
She tempers down the thunder,
Lays serene, so serene.
She ripples through the river,
She shoots down the sky,
She holds all your silent prayers —
You couldn't know why.
She wipes your tears,
She cradles your pain,
She wrecks the path, you'd never walk again.
And when you fall on her lap,

You find her love so dense,
For you to live a life,
Fluent in silence.

23. Dear Diary

Dear Diary,
Since the last time I stared at the clock,
I've been bleeding.
I've tried sleeping, weeping, keeping my serenity to myself,
Yet it won't stop bleeding.
But you don't have a say in going,
But going far away where the clock won't tick anymore,
Would not take the bleeding away.
Keeping at bay,
Having so much to feel but little to say,
Dear Diary, you will never hear from me again.
But there are many pages left to pen down,
Many rights to wright,
Many wrongs to repent at night,
Dear Diary, you will remain underneath my tear-blurred sight.
I shall cover you up in leather,
Paint you green and brown till I go blue,
Maybe my loved one's start missing me,

But Dear Diary, won't you?
You hear what I can't comprehend,
The desires of this materialistic plane.
You, choose to rather mend,
A part of me that I can't shed.
'Cause Dear Diary, for you it's only me,
Good, bad, better, worse, whatever,
But me.
You hold me like a naked soul,
You have my selfish desires,
My spoiled toxicity,
It's these things you behold.
Good one's you let me spread,
Bad one's you keep in shade,
Dear Diary, you're aubade.
So when you stop hearing from me,
Burn down your pages,
Sink in an old well full of moss,
Don't let my strings strum at any cost,
'Cause Dear Diary, as a friend, you must.
Oh Dear Diary,
But when I melt into a flare star,
And you see me shine,
I promise, I'll brighten up your night,
Light down into the well,
Stay till twilight.
I'll dance around the cosmos,

Dwindle around the moon,
Whisk away all the darkness,
Will grow wise and true.
So when the clock stops ticking,
And you feel the warmth of my palms cease,
Look for me up in those flares,
Where I found peace.
And when the twilight sets,
To the waters, when all the seashells flow,
And you don't ever hear from me again,
Dear Diary, let me go.

www.ingramcontent.com/pod-product-compliance
Lightning Source LLC
Chambersburg PA
CBHW070458050426
42449CB00012B/3026